be outstanding

How To Achieve Outstanding Lessons Under The New Ofsted Framework

(2014 Edition)

By KJ O'Hara

Contents

Forward

Since September 2006 I have worked as a leader in schools in Special Measures and Notice to Improve. During that time I have been subject to over 20 Ofsted and Local Authority inspections. In my last post, as Assistant Headteacher with responsibility for Teaching and Learning, the methods I discuss in this book helped raise the percentage of teaching graded good or better from 4o% to 82% in just 9 months and helped the school get out of Special Measures, under the new Ofsted Framework, in just 15 months.

The book that follows highlights the key elements in classroom teaching that my colleagues and I implemented and developed in order to dramatically raise the standards of teaching across the school in such a short time. During that time, the majority of teachers who had consistently been getting satisfactory in their observations moved to at least good and many of them achieved outstanding. I hope that by reading this book you can do the same.

Introduction

There is no magic formula for an outstanding lesson. If you plan the same lesson for two similar classes one may be judged outstanding whilst the other may fail miserably. What is planned on paper and prepared for in advanced does not guarantee success – it's all about what happens in the classroom.

The aim of this book, therefore, is not to give you a formula, a lesson structure or a planning frame, but to give you help with implementing the 'best practice' needed to meet the criteria for outstanding under the current Ofsted Framework. Before discussing that practice, it's important that you have a clear idea of exactly what inspectors (and senior leaders) are now judging when they observe your lesson.

The New Ofsted Framework

Under the new framework inspectors are giving a judgement on three separate elements of a lesson. These are:

1) the behaviour of students in the lesson

2) the progress of students over time

3) the quality of teaching

1) The Behaviour of Students

Many teachers and particularly NQTs mistakenly think that inspectors are judging how well behaved the students are in lessons. The focus of these teachers is on making sure there is no disruption, that work is undertaken quietly and that children are on task.

Whilst lack of disruption and being on task are important, these are not the ingredients of an outstanding lesson. What inspectors are looking for is that the behaviour of children actually contributes to the learning taking place in the lesson. They want to see enthusiasm, genuine engagement with tasks and real co-operation between students where they work together to solve problems and help each other progress; in their own words 'a high level of commitment to learning.'

Simply having them not disrupting and being on task will not achieve this. As for working quietly, that all depends on the task, but a noisy, chaotic classroom full of busy children can be evidence of superb engagement with plenty of learning and progress taking place.

2) Progress over time

This new area of judgement has been an Achilles' heel for many teachers since the new framework was introduced. I recall doing a joint observation with an inspector of a teacher who had consistently achieved outstanding under the previous framework and whilst the lesson itself was, under the old framework, still outstanding, the inspector would only grade progress over time as 'not good, needs improvement' because of the poor quality of the work and the marking and assessment seen in books.

The implication of this is that to achieve outstanding you can no longer get away with performing less well throughout the year and then put on a 'show lesson' when you are being observed. Inspectors will look at the previous work of the students and will want to see that the quality of the students' work has been consistently good; that there has been rapid and sustained progress across almost the entire class; that the work given is challenging and shows you have high expectations; and that the books are marked regularly with constructive comments that give clear guidance on what the student needs to do to progress. They are also keen that students are given timely feedback, so that the comments made by teachers are given within a time frame which will be useful.

For those teachers who use the old trick of hiding their books during inspections and using paper and worksheets, this is no longer a viable option as inspectors will ask to see the work after the observation had finished. If you can't provide it, then there is no evidence of progress over time and therefore it gets a grading of inadequate.

3) The quality of teaching

Inspectors tend to believe that if the quality of teaching is consistently good or better than both behaviour and progress over time will also be good or better. If you have a class where pupils are continually unenthusiastic, don't cooperate and make poor progress, it's going to be difficult to get them to raise their game for a single lesson just because you are being observed. It will show.

The first real tip for getting outstanding lessons, therefore, has to be this: you have to be consistently trying to deliver outstanding lessons; you can no longer get away with a one off super lesson.

What constitutes outstanding teaching is less easy to summarise, but in general they are looking for the following:

a) that you have a thorough understanding of the abilities of all the children in your class, their strengths, weaknesses, prior learning, working at levels, targets and special needs;

b) that you use the data above to provide work which is differentiated for students of differing abilities; that you have **consistently high expectations**; and you provide work at a level that challenges all students to **make rapid and sustained progress**.

c) that you support students with specific needs (e.g. special needs, pupil premium, EAL etc.) to make **rapid and sustained progress**;

d) that you use **well-judged and imaginative teaching strategies** to **engage students** to participate enthusiastically and help challenge them to progress;

e) that during the lesson progress has been made by all students and that **almost all are making rapid and sustained progress**;

f) that **during a lesson** you systematically and effectively **check students' understanding** and **make appropriate intervention** where needed to rectify errors and ensure progress continues.

g) that the teaching of **reading, writing, communication and maths** is addressed where required and appropriate, regardless of the subject being taught;

h) that marking is of a high quality with timely, constructive feedback that leads to rapid progress.

It's possible to add to this list, but essentially these are the core elements that inspectors will be looking to see.

With the new framework there are some things which have gone out of favour, one significant difference is that it's no longer necessary to deliver a three-part, 'starter, main, plenary' lesson. You can do if it is needed, but it's not compulsory. In fact, the updated Ofsted Inspection Handbook published in January 2014, states, **'Inspectors must not expect teaching staff to teach in any specific way. Schools and teachers should decide for themselves how to teach.'**

Another area of change is that inspectors are no longer much interested in your lesson plan, indeed, as you are expected to **systematically and effectively check students' understanding and make appropriate intervention**, an outstanding teacher would be expected to abandon the lesson plan and readdress the areas where intervention is required in order to ensure progress continues. Sticking to a lesson plan that's not working just because you have given it to an observer is not therefore a good thing – it's all about you judging what is happening in the lesson itself, not what's written on the plan. Just have the confidence in your own ability to do this.

Think of a lesson like a journey: if you'd planned your route and half way through you had a flat tyre you wouldn't continue driving, you'd stop and fix the problem. It's the same with your plan for the child's learning journey – this is what an inspector would look to see an outstanding teacher doing.

Data, High Expectations and Challenge

Using data effectively is the real key to outstanding teaching. The reason for this is quite simple: in order to make rapid and sustained progress, students need work which is challenging. Challenging work shows that the teacher has high expectations – but the only way to ensure you have high expectations and that the work is genuinely challenging is use the data to pitch the work at the right level for the needs of individual students.

If expected progress at secondary school is three levels, (a student arriving at level 5 should be expected to achieve grade B at GCSE) then the high expectation and challenge is to try to get that student to achieve grade A or A*. If that student is currently working at grade C and is doing work which will not get them above grade C, the observer is not going to be able to say you have high expectations or that the work is truly challenging. No matter how well they do during that lesson, at the end of it they will not have progressed beyond the level which they started the lesson.

By using data effectively, you will know the working at and target levels for the children in your class and can then plan work which is above their working at level and heading towards or beyond their targets. Students working at the top of level five should be given work which will allow them to achieve level 6. Even if they do not achieve it, they are still being challenged to do so and will be making progress towards it. It's the 'making progress' that inspectors are interested in.

To make it obvious that you have high expectations and are challenging the students, have a sheet with your students' data printed out to give to an observer / inspector. This will indicate to them that you know your students' abilities. Follow this up by having **levelled learning outcomes** for the lesson and introduce them in a challenging way: 'For those of you working at level 4, I want you to achieve learning outcome 2 today, which is at level 5. Let's see how many of you can get there!' Speaking like this to the class is a challenge in itself and clearly lets the observer know you have expectations that they should try to progress beyond their current level.

Differentiation

The most effective way you use data is in setting work according to the ability of students in your class. However, all classes have students of differing abilities and outstanding teachers will provide work which is differentiated for students of differing abilities.

Using data, divide every class into three broad groups: High Ability, Middle Ability and Lower Ability. (You should even do this in setted groups, so if you have a top GCSE group your higher ability students could be those targeted grade A*, your middle ability students those targeted grade A and your lower ability those targeted grade B.) Make sure that on the data sheet you hand over to the observer, that it is clear which students are in each group.

Differentiation by content, process and product

Many teachers were taught to differentiate by task or by outcome. A better way to think about differentiation is by thinking about content, process and product.

Content

Basically this means that the content of your lesson is different for each ability group. For example, if an English teacher were asking students to look at a scene from a Shakespeare play, the lower ability group might read a scene transcribed into modern day

English, the middle ability group might be given the original text with margin notes, whilst the higher ability group could just be given the original text without the notes.

In a history lesson looking at reign of Henry VIII, the lower ability group might look at biographies of the King's life, the middle ability might be looking at the changes taking place within religion and the higher group might be looking at how religious beliefs affected the political landscape of the country.

In a maths lesson covering equations, a teacher may provide graded worksheets, each of differing level of challenge. Students can start at a level suitable to them and then progress upwards as they complete each worksheet.

Differentiation by content, therefore, means providing different resources for students of different ability to work on. It can also mean they may be working on different aspects of a theme or topic from other members of the class.

Process

Process refers to the activities children undertake to learn. So, for example, in a KS2 science lesson looking at how plants grow, the lower ability students might learn by playing an interactive game where they water and a plant and put it out in the sunshine. The middle ability group may watch a video about how water and light affect plant growth, the higher ability students might undertake an experiment with plants, feeding them differing amounts of water, putting them in differently lit places and subjecting them to different temperatures.

In a PSCHE class about bullying, the lower ability students could create a survey about bullying, the middle ability groups could interview people about bullying and the higher ability group could create a role-play about the effects of bullying.

In these examples, the content is still the same, but the process by which each group learns is different.

Product

The product is the final result of the learning – the finished piece of work. In a KS2 group studying a class reader, for example, there may be some children who can write well and others who can barely write at all. In this situation you could have the final piece of work of the lower ability students to be a recorded video of them answering questions about the text. The middle ability group could produce PowerPoint presentation with images and some text whilst the higher ability group could be asked to produce an extended piece of writing.

In maths lesson about 3d shapes the lower ability group could be asked to create 3D shapes using modelling equipment, the middle ability group could be asked to provide a wall display of different shapes labelled with their attributes and the higher ability group could be asked to write down how they would teach other students about 3d shapes and their attributes.

Again, whilst students are still studying the same theme or topic, the final product that they are aiming to complete is differentiated according to their ability.

It's not necessary to differentiate by content, process and product at the same time and nor is it expected that every single activity in a lesson will be differentiated. The subsidiary guidance for inspectors, published in January 2014, states, **'It is unrealistic, too, for inspectors to necessarily expect that all work in all lessons is always matched to the specific needs of each individual.'** However, every lesson should have some form of differentiated work in it and this is especially so for observed lessons. Make sure that the work is differentiated to challenge the students to achieve higher than their current levels.

Showing Progress

Observers and Inspectors can't see everything that's going on in a lesson and within a few minutes of being in your classroom they will start to focus in on particular things and begin to create their own agenda of what to look for to evidence the judgements they want to make.

One essential skill that the modern teacher needs to have is to 'Narrate the Lesson'. What this means is that you make it perfectly clear to the observer what is going on and draw their attention to what you want them to see. As observations can be as short as 20 minutes, this is especially important if they have missed important elements of your lesson. Narrating the lesson can be undertaken in a number of ways.

1) Narrating to the class

This is basically speaking to the children for the benefit of the observer. So if you see a student or a group of students have made progress in a particular area, you may say to them, 'Well done, you've made good progress there,' and then follow this up with a challenging question such as, 'Now you've done this, how can you make it even better?'

Whilst this helps the students by being both praise and challenge, it will certainly help if the observer or inspector hears you. You won't get credit for saying this, but what will happen is that astute observers should pick up on what you are saying and will go and investigate the progress for themselves. This way, if they are looking for evidence of progress, you have showed them where to find it.

Another way to do this is to explain to the class what you are doing and why you are doing it in a way that will make your lesson look good for the observer. 'Group A, I've given you some questions here which are above your target levels, I'd really like you to challenge yourself and give them a go.' Again, this makes it clearly obvious to an inspector that you have high expectations and are challenging the students.

2) Speak directly to the observer / inspector

Many teachers think that there should be no interaction between them and the observer or inspector during the lesson and that they should focus totally on the teaching. This is quite wrong. Good observers will certainly interact with the students, asking them questions and looking at their work. If there is something good that they have not noticed and you want them to have a look at it, then tell them. 'Can you have a look at the work those students are doing over there, I think you might like it.' Don't get into a ten minute conversation, but politely and quickly guide them to aspects of the learning taking place.

3) Have regular progress checks during the lesson

Regular progress checks are a vital element of outstanding teaching because they are the key to understanding whether or not progress is being made and thus tell you whether you need to halt the lesson plan and readdress problems or misconceptions which are preventing progress from being made. The new Ofsted Inspection Handbook lists under its grade criteria for outstanding: **'Teachers systematically and effectively check pupils' understanding throughout lessons, anticipating where they may need to intervene and doing so with notable impact on the quality of learning.'**

When it is apt to do so, stop your pupils from working and ask them what progress they have made so far.

'Group 3, I asked you to look at causes of WW1, what progress have you made so far? ... Good, what are you going to do next and why?'

The students' responses here are evidence of progress that the observer cannot ignore – especially if you are using terms like: 'What progress have you made?' or 'What have you learned that you didn't know before?'

Where you discover students are not making progress, you put yourself in a position where you can intervene effectively. You've found this out during the lesson and not at the end so you can now address the problems and enable them to progress as the lesson continues. When you do your next progress check, ten minutes later, start with the groups that were struggling during the last progress check. 'Okay group 2, you were struggling the last time, what progress have you made since I explained it to you?

A few words of advice here:

a) Keep the progress checks short and snappy – no more than a minute, the emphasis is on keeping the children learning and whilst checking progress is important if it goes on for too long, it can halt the learning process.

b) Avoid progress checks that do not realistically check progress. I have seen Ofsted inspectors criticise the use of techniques like thumbs up if you understand and thumbs down if you don't or pupils holding up red, yellow and green cards to signify how well they are doing. The reason Ofsted do not like these is because they are not considered genuine AFL (Assessment for Learning) techniques. Pupils might not want to publicly show they are struggling so may put a thumbs up just so they don't look silly in front of their friends, others might genuinely think they are doing well when they are not.

Instead, you need to **use good questioning skills**, asking the children 'What progress...' 'Tell me three things...' 'Explain what it is you have done...' etc. that will establish whether they are making progress or not. This even gives you chance to turn problems into solutions. 'Okay, so that hasn't worked for you. Can you think of another way you can look at the problem in order to find a solution?' or 'What have you done that hasn't worked? Is there a better or different way?' And always remember the 'How do you make even more progress from here?' or 'What are your next steps?' questions.

c) Some observations can be quite short, so don't go too long without having one. It's always helpful to mark on your lesson plan where you intend to put your progress checks, so even if the inspector doesn't stay around long, they know you have planned them.

4) Engineering Progress

In basic terms, progress can be defined as the difference in learning that a student has made between the start and finish of the lesson.

One technique I have seen many teachers do successfully is to start the lesson by asking students to do something which they know that they will do badly, use this as a starting point for the learning and then show the progression as the lesson continues.

For example, in maths I have seen a teacher start the lesson by asking students to work on an equation that they knew they couldn't answer. The teacher then got the students to look at the mistakes they were making in order to work out the formula for themselves and then, through co-operative learning, they managed to solve the equation later on. As an observer in this lesson, the outcome to me was obvious – at the beginning no-one could work it out, at the end everyone could – progress!

In another example, I have seen a drama teacher start off a lesson by getting students to perform a section of a play they had never seen before. The performances were quite poor but were the stimulus for the acting groups to first discuss the meaning of text and, one by one, to work on developing voice, movement and characterisation. After each stage of the lesson the group were asked to re-enact the scene – the progression could be seen continuously after the students added skill after skill to developing the performance.

As the teacher stopped for a progress check every 15 minutes and there was progress at every check, it was made clear that the progress was rapid and sustained – a clear requirement for outstanding.

What both teachers had done here was to 'engineer progress' through the structure of the lesson. I do need to point out here that this was done for the benefit of the students and to aid the learning and not merely to make it look good for the observer – however, it did look good as the progress was obvious in both instances. Both lessons were judged outstanding.

Progress Over Time

To evidence sustained progress, inspectors, more than ever before, want to look at students' work - so have the evidence there for the observer to see.

If your students' work doesn't show progress over time then there is nothing you can do here. However, it is also possible that if your students have made progress over time that it will not be obvious to the inspector or observer.

There is an easy solution to this, have your students' work available for them to see. Although they might be using their current book in the lesson, you may also have previous books, coursework folders, portfolios, wall displays or other evidence for them to see. Have this ready for them and don't be afraid to say to them, 'If you want to see progress over time, take a look at this work.'

Although I know teachers already have a massive workload, if you have the time and the inclination, it would be a good idea to put a folder together showing the work of a few children in the class which evidences rapid and sustained progress.

Evidence of the drafting of written work is often an excellent record of how students progress from initial ideas through to the final draft – have these drafts available. In the modern classroom when students tend to work with computers, teachers can often let students overwrite the first draft when redrafting and as a result the proof of progress from one draft to another is lost. It's important, if you do let students do this, to get print outs of plans and drafts so improvements can be shown.

Use Cooperative Strategies In Your Lessons

Co-operative strategies are an essential element of a modern lesson and for several very good reasons. However, many teachers confuse co-operative strategies with 'group work' and whilst there is a lot of group work involved in co-operative strategies, group work itself is a poor relation that does not offer the opportunities for learning that co-operative strategies do. If you want to achieve outstanding, make good use of cooperative strategies.

What are the differences between group work and co-operative strategies?

Group work simply means getting students to work together in groups. Some teachers use this for a variety of reasons, for example, having the class grouped by ability so that work of different levels can be given to different groups or, alternatively, having mixed ability groups where more able students can support the less able. More adventurous teachers also assign roles to different members of the group, such as leader, scribe, fact checker, task timer, etc.

Whilst getting students to work in groups is to be applauded (some teachers find group work too chaotic and others find the lack of control daunting), it has a potential weakness that can seriously impact upon your lesson's grading.

Group work is perfect for those students who want to take time out. They can sit back, let the others in the group do all the work and then copy it up without having the slightest input. With all the noise and activity going on in the classroom it's very easy for these children to be invisible to a teacher who is table hopping or stationed with a support group. It's also possible that what looks like a couple of busy students enthusiastically engaged in a task could quite easily be two off task students enthusiastically discussing the latest video game. Whilst these off task students might be invisible to the teacher, they certainly won't be to the inspector or observer. As far as they will be concerned, both behaviour and progress of these students will be an issue.

Cooperative strategies on the other hand prevent students taking time out because they are structured in such a way that all students are required to participate in the work. Take a simple strategy like 'Think, Pair, Share.' for example. Each student in the pair is given a letter A or B. A and B, individually, have to think of an answer. A must then explain their answer to B and then B must explain their answer to A. A and B must then share their answers with the class. Using this strategy, both students are required to come up with an answer, tell each other and then tell the class. No-one gets to opt out of the work. If you had simply asked them to work as a pair to think of an answer, it's quite possible that this could have been the work of just one of the students, not both.

It's easy to see the benefits here of using a co-operative strategy rather than simply doing 'group work.' Every student is involved and therefore engaged and challenged.

A favourite strategy of mine that works particularly well in observations is the Jigsaw Technique. To explain this let's imagine that we are teaching science, that the question the whole class have to answer is 'Who is the most influential scientist?' and that there are 25 students in the class.

What I like about this co-operative strategy is that the teacher does not have to teach at all and it becomes very apparent to the observer or inspector that all the learning taking place is done by the students teaching themselves.

In this lesson, the teacher would divide the class into five groups of five. Each group has to discuss the merits of five different scientists and put them in a rank order of importance. Each student in the group is given a letter A,B.C.D or E.

As soon as each person is given their letter, the group is immediately split up and 5 new groups are formed. Have all the As in one group, the Bs in another and so forth. In these new groups, all members are given a number 1 to 5. Each person is then given an information sheet or resource about one of the five candidates for most influential scientist. None of the resources are the same, so no student in the new group has the same information as the others.

For the first five minutes of the lesson, the new groups have to work in silence as each member works independently to read through their resource sheets and make notes on things they think are important about their scientist. After this, in turn, person 1 through to 5 has to teach the rest of that group what they have learned about that scientist whilst the others listen and make notes. At the end of this session, each person in the group will have been taught about that single scientist by themselves and four other people and will have quite a lot of information to take back to their original groups.

When back in their original groups, you will have five students who will now be experts on one particular scientist. Their job now, working from person A through to E is to tell the rest of the group what they have learned about their scientist and for the rest to make notes on what the others have said.

At the end of this exercise, each group will have learned about all five scientists and will be in a position to debate which scientists should be put in which order. First they order them individually, then as a group they explain to each other why they have ranked them in the way they have. Their penultimate task is to come up with a group answer.

Finally, as a plenary, each group is to explain who their most important scientist was and give their reasons.

An outstanding teacher would take this further and ensure that the resources were differentiated, so that the more able students were given more complex texts and that the tasks were differentiated too, perhaps with less able groups just be required to pick their most important scientist whilst more able groups being required to rank all five.

Try to imagine what an observer would see in this lesson. From a starting point of total ignorance each student learns about five important scientists and, by the end of the lesson, is able to make evaluative judgements about their importance. This has been done without any 'from the front' teaching input from the teacher themselves, it has all come from the students being actively engaged in differentiated work. As the activity is a cooperative strategy, all students have taken part and have cooperated in helping themselves and each other. From both a behavioural and teaching point of view, this is a perfect strategy to help you achieve an outstanding lesson.

The Jigsaw Technique can easily be adapted for all kinds of subjects and you can play around with group sizes and numbers of groups to match the size of your own groups.

There are many different types of cooperative strategy and depending upon the content of your lesson, there is bound to be one which can be used. There are many books and websites that can give you detailed information on these without me having to elaborate here. However, my personal favourite is the Northern Ireland Curriculum's *Active Learning and Teaching Methods for Key Stage 3.'* Despite the title, it's equally as useful for all key stages. A search for Kagan Structures is also useful.

A helpful tip for when you do cooperative strategies in groups is to display the groupings on the whiteboard so students don't have to ask which group they are in or where they are sitting. This can save many minutes of valuable learning time. It's also helpful, if you have done this, to check the register prior to the beginning of the lesson in case some students are absent and you need to modify the groupings before the lesson begins.

A word of warning

It's easy, when observing a lesson, to tell when the class has never done group work or cooperative strategies before. Where it is done regularly the students know what is happening – they know the name of the strategy, what it involves, where to sit, who with, what the rules are, what their roles are, etc. As they know what is happening, the transition from a whole class introduction to a group work activity is quick, slick and relatively unchaotic.

Working with other students is also a social skill that doesn't come easy to all students in a class. When you first begin to work using these techniques there will be issues: boys and girls may not want to mix and even if you put them in the same group they might not work well together to start with: a group of four with two boys and two girls may try to work as two gender pairs rather than as a team of four. It takes time and practice to develop good group working skills. There will be other students who simply do not like other members of the group and refuse to cooperate with them – make it easy on yourself, just keep them apart.

It can take a while to break down these barriers and establish working groups, roles and practices so that things run smoothly. If doing this for the first time or if it was something you only did very rarely, it's likely that setting up the activity and explaining what the work is would take overlong and be chaotic with some of students still being unclear of exactly what they were doing and requiring the further explanation even as the activity was being carried out.

As a result of the chaos and loss of time, attempting to do group work or cooperative strategies for the first time during an observation is just asking for trouble. Spending too much time organising and explaining means that little time will be available for actual learning and making progress and you will be setting yourself up for an inadequate judgement. It also makes it obvious that you are someone who doesn't normally utilise group work or cooperative strategies in your lessons – which again does not paint a favourable picture.

The advice, therefore, is to begin using cooperative strategies in your lessons as soon as possible and make them a regular feature of your teaching repertoire. However, if you have never used them with that particular class, I don't recommend using them in an observation.

Independent Work

There has been a big emphasis recently on increasing the amount of independent learning taking place in lessons. Some senior leadership teams have tried to make it a compulsory aspect of lessons in their school. However, the January 2014 revised guidance to Ofsted Inspectors states, **'Do not expect to see 'independent learning' in all lessons and do not make the assumption that this is always necessary or desirable.'**

That said, independent learning is a vital part of modern teaching and planning time for it in lessons is a very useful way to demonstrate that your students have mastered or are developing the learning skills that Ofsted are looking for, these being: **'engagement, interest, concentration, determination, resilience and independence.'** (Ofsted School Inspection Handbook, Jan 2014).

I wouldn't, however, devote an entire observed lesson to independent learning, but instead would make it part of the mix of activities I was arranging, for example, using it prior to cooperative work, so that students have something to take to the discussions that they will take part in, or giving time after the cooperative strategies so that they can use what they have learned in the group work to write up their own conclusions in preparation for a plenary.

Questioning

Questioning is a skill that is specifically mentioned in the Jan 2014 Ofsted School Inspection Handbook: '**teachers use questioning and discussion to assess the effectiveness of their teaching and promote pupils' learning**'. From what is written, it looks clear that inspectors are looking at two separate functions of questioning: using it to assess progress made in the lesson and using it to develop further learning.

I have already discussed its usefulness for assessment under the section dealing with progress checks so will not repeat that here, however, with regard to using questioning to promote learning there are two successful approaches I think need discussing in more detail, these are: Bloom's (Revised) Taxonomy and funnelling techniques.

Bloom's (Revised) Taxonomy should be familiar to most teachers, so I won't go on at length. In essence, Bloom's is a hierarchical list of thinking skills. At the bottom there are basic skills such remembering and understanding, in the centre are applying and analysing and at the top, evaluating and creating.

To challenge students and promote learning, it is best to ask students questions which require the higher order thinking skills at the top of the Bloom's hierarchy. So instead of asking students what happened in Act 1 Scene 1 of Richard III which, as a remembering question, is a low level thinking skill, a more challenging question would be to ask them to evaluate how successful the scene is at introducing us to the character of Richard.

An even more successful approach that inspectors and observers like to see is to combine the use of Bloom's with the funnelling technique. Funnelling is the art of asking three or four questions, starting off with a closed question at the bottom of the Bloom's hierarchy and, from there, moving upwards with more open and challenging questions which require higher order thinking skills. For example:

1. What is the capital of England?
2. Why are capital cities important?
3. Which other cities in England would make a good capital city?

Rather than ask this to several students, ask it of one student. Then observers can see this student's upward journey through the learning curve. Progress!

Don't spend too long on whole class questioning. As it's a 'one student at a time' exercise, the whole class are not fully involved and so the learning process can be halted. If it goes on for a long time some students can lose interest and be off task. Keep your whole class questioning time to a bare minimum, only a minute or two at most, give thinking time before asking for an answer and, to make sure every student is kept focused, insist on a 'no hands up' policy. You choose who is going to answer. (Again, showing high expectations and challenge to all.)

Personally, I prefer to question students individually or in small groups whilst the others are involved in another learning activity. Here you can focus specifically on those students and their needs and have a much better assessment of how well they are progressing.

If you want to show off your questioning skills to the inspector, pick a student or group of students sat near to the inspector and question them whilst the inspector is in earshot.

Pace

Pace has two meanings in education: pace of progress and pace of the lesson and each needs discussing separately.

Pace of the Lesson

What observers are really interested in here is not how quickly things are done, but how wisely time is used. There are some teachers who wrongfully presume that everything has to be done quickly, that every activity must have a time limit and then you need to move on. This however, does not cater for the needs of individual students, some of whom will grasp ideas easily and move on at speed whilst others will need more time to develop the same skills or complete their tasks. Also, some tasks take more time to complete successfully than others.

More importantly, a teacher needs to ensure that as much time in the lesson is used for learning as possible and that there is as little dead time as can be managed. Ensuring this happens is not down to timing skills but more a result of how prepared and organised the teacher is.

Excellent tips to ensure a pacy lesson

1) Bell work.

Have work for the students to do as soon as they enter the room. It can be put up on a whiteboard or handed to the student as a printed sheet as soon as they arrive. Give them a short time limit for this and ensure the instructions are clear. It needs only be a simple or preparatory task, such as matching up key words needed for the lesson to their definitions, but it means the students who enter the class first are not waiting around for others or you before they begin learning. It also helps set the working tone for the lesson as there is no need to settle the class before work starts and it also has the benefit of giving you time to take a register and sort out any issues such as students who have forgot books or pens before you begin the main part of the lesson.

Make the bell work a relevant part of the lesson and spend a minute checking on progress at the end of the task before moving on.

It's always better if the students are in the habit of doing this rather than it being done for the first time when you are observed.

2) Have copious amounts of extension work available for those who finish quickly.

Some students always finish before the others. If these students are sat around doing nothing whilst you wait for the stragglers to finish, then the pace of progress for those students is not going to be judged good and it's likely they will end up disrupting the rest of the class who are still working. Instead, have extension work available for them that you can hand out easily. Extension work does not mean more of the same; it means harder, more challenging work. If they have sailed easily through what you have already given them, it's not going to benefit them to do more of the same – it needs to be harder.

3) Stop yourself from being the biggest time waster in the class

Frequently when I've observed lessons the major cause of poor pace has been the teacher themselves. If you are spending 10 or 15 minutes at the beginning of the lesson talking to the class, explaining the tasks in too much detail or over emphasising the learning outcomes then 25% of the learning time of the lesson is being wasted.

I am not stating here that you should not take some time to introduce the topic or explain some terms to the class and even the new Ofsted Subsidiary Guidance (Jan 2014) states that inspectors **'should not criticise teacher talk for being overlong ... unless there is unequivocal evidence that this is slowing learning over time.'** However, the term 'overlong' speaks for itself.

Be succinct. Keep explanations of your learning outcomes brief (never waste time getting students to copy them out) and keep your instructions simple, minimal and always visible on the whiteboard so you don't have to keep repeating them. Once you have given them, check who understands and if someone doesn't then deal with them individually so those who do know what they are doing can get started.

4) A better way of learning

One excuse that teachers often use when they are criticised for spending too much time talking at the front is that they needed to teach something before the students could do the work. For example, before getting students to write a poem using metaphors, they spend 20 minutes at the front explaining what metaphors are.

A better and more imaginative teaching strategy would be to give students tasks which allow them to discover for themselves what metaphors are without you having to deliver it through teacher talk. This would create a much more enjoyable, challenging and engaging lesson with more emphasis on independent learning instead of being 'taught' in the old fashioned sense.

Pace of Progress

Pace of progress is different to the pace of the lesson. It's not about how time is utilised in the lesson, but about how quickly students learn and make progress. Inspectors will already know, before they enter the school, how good your students' progress is in comparison to local and national averages. They will want to find out how your students' progress compares to other students in the school or in comparison to other subjects. If you teach maths and all your students are at level 4 in your subject but are at level 5 in English, then the inspector will want to investigate why. Similarly if the local or national average is level 5 they will want to know why your students are a level lower. They will also have access to your schools' internal data, showing how far and how quickly these students have progressed since they arrived. Part of what they are doing is judging whether what appears in the data is backed up by what they see in the classroom. If your assessment data shows consistent progress over time, but the lesson observation shows this does not happen in lessons, then they will be less likely to trust the school's data and this in turn can have a big impact on the judgement they make for leadership and management of the school.

To award outstanding, inspectors will want to see, by the end of the lesson, that all students have made progress and almost all have made good progress.

They will evidence this by:

1. Talking to the students about the work they are doing
2. Scrutinising their work and books
3. Listening to them talk to each other
4. Listening to them answer your questions
5. Seeing how well they progress with the tasks they are given
6. Making judgments about how challenging the work you give them is

A good way of ensuring that pace of progress has been good is by getting them to show they can transfer those skills to use in a different way or show they understand the principals behind what they have learned. If they have learned to identify and name different prisms, get them to write their own definitions of what a prism is. If they have learned to write the opening of an adventure story, ask them what they might do if they were writing the opening of a horror story? If you have taught them to make a Tenon joint in technology ask them where they would use a Tenon joint if they were going to build something.

Behaviour

I've already mentioned that what inspectors are really looking for in an outstanding lesson is cooperative behaviour which contributes to the learning, rather than simply having well behaved students. The Ofsted Framework states that inspectors are looking to see that: **'teachers and other adults create a positive climate for learning in which pupils are interested and engaged.'** If you are regularly using cooperative strategies in lessons and your lessons are engaging this should be apparent in how your students behave in lessons.

However, there are always students who are having a bad day or who are going to be challenging and there are measures you should take to make sure that both behaviour and teacher-pupil relationships are seen in a positive light.

Follow the school policy

Inspectors will be very keen to see whether individual teachers correctly follow the school's disciplinary procedures. It is essential that whatever the school's policy is, that you follow it. This is difficult to do if you don't normally do it and try to follow it just because you are being observed. If your disciplinary routines are different from the school's your students will have a different set of behavioural expectations in your lessons. If you try to tighten up behaviour by suddenly switching to the school policy, the students will react against you. I have frequently had to cringe in observations when teachers, trying to apply the school disciplinary policy, are heckled by their students with comments such as, 'You never do this when you're not being observed!' Once again, you need to establish a routine before the inspection takes place and follow school policy in order to show the observer that you have high expectations of behaviour and apply school policy consistently.

Interestingly enough, one group of teachers who are particularly bad at following school discipline procedure are senior leaders. As their position in the school means they don't have usually have the discipline issues other members of staff do, they often do not adhere to school policy. However, when Ofsted arrive, it is still very obvious in observations that they are not using it.

Meet and greet

One of the best ways to ensure that there is a congenial atmosphere in the classroom before the lesson starts is to meet students at the door. Doing this allows you to make sure the students are in the right frame of mind before the lesson starts. Have them line up quietly and say good morning to them as they enter. Not only does this set the correct tone for the lesson, it also gives you chance to sort out any little issues such as uniform or equipment before the student enters the room.

Don't underestimate the importance of this; it's quite common for the first five minutes of a lesson to be completely wasted by teachers having to sort out students who fail to come to lesson properly equipped. If this were to happen in every lesson in a school with a 25 period week then that class loses over 16 days of education over a year. That's half a year's schooling in primary.

Imagine the progress students could make at the end of Key Stage2 or Key Stage 4 if you could give them another half a year's teaching?

From a disciplinary point of view, a sloppy start to the lesson is to be frowned upon. Whilst you are trying to solve the little issues of a small number of students, the rest of the class are hanging around waiting. They get restless, they begin conversations, some of them begin acting silly and this unsettled beginning can set a slow fuse burning. The focus moves away from learning and you need to settle the whole class down to get order before you begin. You may even need to raise your voice to get everyone's attention.

To solve this, ensure you have spare pens, rulers, rubbers pencils, paper and whatever else they need available for your lesson easily accessible so that they don't even need to ask you for it. If students have any other issues send them away and tell them you'll deal with it once the class have begun their work.

Praise frequently

Praise is a major factor in motivating students, making them feel valued and in encouraging desired behaviour. It's easy to give and works wonders. Praise students for aspects of good behaviour: wearing correct uniform, settling down quickly, working well in groups, doing good work – and keep praising all the way through the lesson. If someone has been reprimanded, quietly praise them if they have made an improvement to keep them motivated. If your school has a rewards system, then use it – indeed, be seen to use it during an observation.

Praise is also an excellent alternative to reprimanding. If you are lining the students up outside and waiting for them to quiet down before letting them in, rather than telling the noisy ones to be quiet, try praising those who have lined up quietly instead. Once you start praising one student you get the domino effect, the others follow very quickly. This way you can even get to praise the potentially naughty students before they enter the room and put them in a more engaging and positive mood for the rest of the lesson.

Reprimand privately

The single most important thing when having to reprimanding students, particularly when you are being observed, is not to let the rest of the class, or even of the student being reprimanded, stop learning.

If a student is off task, the first technique you should use before reprimanding them is 'positive redirection'. In other words, rather than focus on what they are not doing, focus on what they should be doing, for example, 'You made a reasonable start, I think you can do even better if you talked a little less.' 'Have you finished all five questions yet?' 'Don't get behind by talking; you are doing really well, so far.'

If positive direction hasn't had an impact, then progress to a quiet reprimand, preferably out of earshot of the other students. Doing it quietly is much more effective than telling off in public which attracts the attention and distracts other students. It also prevents the reprimanded student from being publicly embarrassed to which they may react negatively. If poor behaviour continues, follow the school procedures, but again, keep it private and quiet.

If necessary, take them to the door, stand them outside so other students cannot see them, (keep the door open so that you can still see the rest of the class) and talk to them there. Do not leave them outside as they will not make any progress or learn anything and this will affect the judgement the observer makes. If they are seriously disrupting, then follow the school procedures for having them removed.

If you need to have a student removed, make sure you do not make a big issue out of it or cause it to disrupt the rest of the lesson. Just deal with it as quickly and quietly as you can. If all your reprimands have been quietly whispered, it's likely you can get rid of the student without everyone else in the lesson needing to find out.

Shouting at a student and making a public show of removing them during an observation can have drastic effect on the lesson. The rest of the class will be disrupted, some will want to talk about it and will have to be brought back to task, others may want to challenge your decision and, as I've seen on several awkward occasions, some friends of the removed student may vent their anger by telling the observer how bad a teacher they think you are. This is certainly not going to get you an outstanding lesson.

If other students do challenge your decision, do not get into a discussion or argument with them, refuse to get drawn into it and get straight back to the lesson and start praising those students who do as you ask.

Literacy and Numeracy

A significant difference between the new Ofsted Framework and its predecessors is the focus on literacy and numeracy. The January 2014 Ofsted Inspection Handbook states that in an outstanding school the teaching of '**reading, writing, communication and mathematics is highly effective and cohesively planned and implemented across the curriculum.**' The key words here are 'across the curriculum'. It is now the responsibility of all teachers to teach literacy and numeracy in all subjects. The biggest impact of this is no doubt in secondary schools where previously it had been mainly left to the English and maths departments.

It is not expected in secondary schools that you need to be a literary or mathematics expert and you would not be expected to be au fait with all the grammatical or mathematical jargon and the like that subject specialists would. However there are certain expectations of all staff, these in the main are that you would:

1) teach key terms and spellings in your subject

2) teach students the forms of writing required in your particular subject (instructions, essays, memos, scientific reports, letters, project briefs, menus, etc.)

3) address basic literacy errors in students writing, (spelling, punctuation, paragraphing, basic grammar etc.)

4) address basic errors in pupil speech (non-standard English, grammatical errors, etc.)

5) model good literacy in both your written instructions and vocal communication

6) give students opportunity to read appropriately challenging literature specific to the subject you are teaching.

7) teach, where necessary, the mathematical skills required in your subjects, such as weighing ingredients, measuring resistant materials, creating geographical graphs or recording historical data.

For literacy, I would recommend that you have three resources available in your class:

a) A word wall which has key words for the subject or theme you are teaching, together with their definitions clearly visible for all.

b) A literacy table mat on the desk in front of all students on which is printed: the basic rules for punctuation; commonly used subject specific terms; connectives to help extended writing and develop thinking skills; and a guide on how to answer specific types of questions. Students should be directed to use these throughout the lesson when appropriate.

c) A collection of writing frames to show students how to structure longer pieces of writing that you may use in the subject, together with help on how to begin and structure the paragraphing in them. In my last school, we used English specialists to help departments create these. If you work in a secondary school and need help, ask your English department or ask your CDP co-ordinator to arrange training for you.

Similarly, if you are teaching mathematics in a non-maths subject, then having resources with formulas, measuring charts, instructions how to read charts, graphs and data etc. is a valuable way that you can address numeracy in your lessons.

If you are observed teaching a non-English or non-maths lesson it is not a requirement that you build literacy or maths teaching into your lesson unless it is required to meet the aim of your learning outcome. If you are an English teacher, there's no need to get students drawing a graph comparing the number of adjectives in a poem's stanzas just for the sake of offering a bit of numeracy. However, it is essential that you are seen to address literacy and mathematical errors such as: correcting the way students speak, addressing mathematical misconceptions and ensuring literacy and maths are addressed when you mark their work.

What helps make the lesson outstanding is if you are seen to use the resources mentioned above when students are working. Even referring to them can help. 'Don't forget to check the word wall for the correct spellings!' 'Before drawing your graph, let's check that we know which is the x and which is the y axis.' 'This report on Henry VIII is to be factual, so we are going to write it in the third person. Who can explain what third person writing is?' Even better, you could model a good answer and draw their attention to the literacy and numeracy skills needed as you do so.

By doing this, you are showing that you are developing the use of literacy and numeracy in your subject and in the school as a whole. This is a significant factor in ensuring that students make sustained progress. Having done observations where I've shadowed specific students throughout a school day to see their learning experiences across the curriculum, it's always been apparent that they tend to leave many of their literacy and numeracy skills in the English and maths classrooms. A student who can write at level 6 in an English classroom can often write at a much lower level in other subjects.

They have lower expectations of themselves when it comes to literacy and numeracy in other subjects and, consequently, the teachers in those other subjects tend to have lower expectations of that student too. As a result, the quality of the students' work can be poorer than it would be if the focus on those skills was addressed more rigorously across the school.

I've also seen this happen in primary schools, where students move from one subject to another without moving classrooms. In a literacy lesson they focus on literacy skills like punctuation, but ten minutes later, sat in the same seat and with the same teacher, they can answer a history question without using a single mark of punctuation in their answers. Within primary schools, the need is to deconstruct the compartmentalisation of subjects in the minds of both students and teachers. Thematic teaching can be a good way to address this, but at the end of the day, it's the teacher's job to ensure that literacy and numeracy skills are hammered home in all lessons.

Conclusion

As I mentioned at the beginning, there is no magic formula for outstanding. However, what I have included here are the elements, methods and techniques which I have consistently seen lead to teachers being awarded an outstanding judgement by Ofsted inspectors.

If you take anything from this book, then let it be this: Ofsted Inspectors are well trained, very experienced and shrewd professionals; you can't easily pull the wool over their eyes. They can quickly spot when a teacher is trying to do something for the first time in a lesson whilst attempting to make out it is a normal element of their teaching. Many of the things I have suggested using to achieve an outstanding grade can only truly work if they are a regular element of your teaching. You need to begin implementing them now so, that by the time you get an inspection, or by the time your next lesson observation takes place, your students know the routines and practices you employ. The days of pulling out your highly polished special lesson for a one off observation are over under the new framework.

Good luck and keep persevering - one small step at a time and you'll get there.